The Rise of Anime and Manga

INTRODUCTION TO ANIME AND MANGA

From Magical Girls to Pirate Kings

MARI BOLTE

TWENTY-FIRST CENTURY BOOKS / MINNEAPOLIS

To all the mangaka whose visions and imaginations have brought light into the world and who have created stories that have brought countless people together—and to all the time and money I've spent on enjoying it

Twenty-First Century Books™
An imprint of Lerner Publishing Group, Inc.
241 First Avenue North
Minneapolis, MN 55401 USA

For reading levels and more information, look up this title at www.lernerbooks.com.

Main body text set in Bembo Std Regular.
Typeface provided by Monotype Typography.

Library of Congress Cataloging-in-Publication Data

Names: Bolte, Mari author
Title: Introduction to anime and manga : from magical girls to pirate kings / Mari Bolte.
Description: Minneapolis : Twenty-First Century Books, 2026. | Series: The rise of anime and manga | Includes bibliographical references and index. | Audience: Ages 11–18 | Audience: Grades 7–9 | Summary: "Anime and manga are a global sensation with millions of fans around the world. Learn what anime and manga are, their popular series, story tropes, genres, and more"—Provided by publisher.
Identifiers: LCCN 2025011272 (print) | LCCN 2025011273 (ebook) | ISBN 9798765662724 library binding | ISBN 9798348029623 paperback | ISBN 9798348000325 epub
Subjects: LCSH: Anime (Motion pictures) | Anime (Television programs) | Manga (Comic books)
Classification: LCC NC1766.J3 B645 2026 (print) | LCC NC1766.J3 (ebook) | DDC 791.43/34—dc23/eng/20250519

LC record available at https://lccn.loc.gov/2025011272
LC ebook record available at https://lccn.loc.gov/2025011273

Manufactured in the United States of America
1 – CG – 12/15/25

CONTENTS

INTRODUCTION

Step into any bookstore, library, or comic book shop and you'll find ever-growing collections of illustrated books and comics, TV shows, and movies from Japan. These shows and movies are called anime, and the illustrated books and comics are manga. Some people think of anime and manga as stories for children, stories about fighting, or stories about heroes. But both have a rich history that has played a huge role in Japan's unique art and storytelling styles.

The word *manga* comes from a combination of kanji, or characters—*man*, which means "whimsical," and *ga*, which means "pictures." Together, the new phrase means "informal drawing." People who write and illustrate their own manga are called mangaka. Japanese manga is traditionally read from right to left, which is how most Japanese is written. Today, most manga are published weekly or monthly, one chapter at a time, and are eventually collected into volumes of several chapters called *tankōbon*.

Anime can mean any kind of cartoons, regardless of their country of origin. But outside of Japan, the word is

Manga stores in Japan sell books from popular publishers.

used to describe Japanese animated movies or TV shows. The word *anime* is a shortened version of "animation." It has been popular in Japan for more than a century and in North America since the 1960s.

Anime and manga are made with many audiences in mind, from small children to serious adults. For example, shojo—which means "young girl" in English—is anime or manga aimed at audiences of young girls ages twelve to eighteen, and josei is aimed at older women around ages eighteen to forty. Similarly, shonen—which means "young boy"—is aimed at young boys ages nine to eighteen, and seinen is aimed at men ages eighteen to forty. But anybody can read or watch shojo, josei, shonen, or seinen. From anime and manga's inception to today, mangaka and filmmakers have pushed the boundaries of what's possible in storytelling, art, technology, and entertainment.

CHAPTER ONE

First, Some Backstory

Manga is an all-encompassing term for comic books and graphic novels that are created in Japan. But it's so much more complex than a collection of illustrated works. It's a lifestyle. In Japan, manga makes up between 35 and 40 percent of all printed and published work. Some people believe that in Japanese, the word *manga* means "curious" or "whimsical picture." Others say that's inaccurate. Either way, manga encompasses comics and graphic novels originating in Japan.

Experts are divided on when the first manga was actually created. Drawings and caricatures have been part of Japanese culture for centuries. Some of the oldest-known comic art was discovered in 1935 during a renovation of the Buddhist Hôryûji Temple in Nara Prefecture. Support beams in the ceiling dating back to 607 CE had caricatures sketched into the wood. But printed and bound manga as we know it today wouldn't exist until much later.

Ukiyo-e prints combine Japan's beauty, nature, and history on one page.

Rise of Print

The early 1700s marked the rise of publishing and books becoming more available to everyone. Ukiyo-e woodblock prints could be mass-produced, which made them much more affordable than individual paintings. Books of ukiyo-e prints called Ehon were made of decorative washi paper and sold in shops. Ehon musha were books inspired by Japanese and Chinese myths, legends, and epic tales. Many modern manga, anime, and even video games combine Ehon musha with Western art styles.

The first reference to manga dates back to 1798 when Kyōden Santō published a picture book called *Shiji no Yukikai*, or *Four Seasons*. Santō had filled the book with drawings of people he saw outside his house. According to historian Eike Exner, Santō used the word *manga* as a verb: "I manga'd those people." This, Exner argues, proves that manga doesn't

Tastes Outside of Japan

During most of the Edo period (1603–1868), the only outside traders allowed in Japan were Dutch. Other traders, such as the Portuguese and Spanish, had tried to convert Japanese people to Christianity. The Dutch didn't, so Japan allowed them to continue trading. Artists in Holland were impressed by the quality of Japan's original works as well as by the quality of their prints.

In 1854, US Navy's Commodore Matthew Perry sailed to Japan. His mission was to open trade with Japan. It is believed that Perry's naval surgeon, Dr. Joseph Wilson, brought a book home with him and translated it. In 1855, the first Japanese book to be reprinted in the United States was an Ehon book.

actually have anything to do with whimsy. Instead, it simply describes sketching or simple drawing.

The famous Japanese artist Katsushika Hokusai (1760–1849) is remembered in modern times for his works including *Great Wave Off Kanagawa* and *Thirty-Six Views of Mount Fuji*. But he also published a book of drawings called the *Hokusai Manga* in 1814. The drawings were playful and humorous. Even though they have no words or stories, they share similarities to the manga of today.

The *Hokusai Manga* was so popular that fourteen more volumes followed. Hokusai's books were a collection of drawings of things that caught his eye—people, animals, or scenes—as well as things that he imagined. Hokusai's manga introduced many Western artists to Japanese art styles. But was the *Hokusai Manga* really the first manga, or did the name

The *Hokusai Manga* was published from 1814–1819 and 1834–1878.

just spread quickly because it was tied to a famous artist? Some argue that it's not manga because Hokusai didn't use his art to tell a story. He just drew whatever he wanted.

Kyōsai Kawanabe signed his paintings "Shōjō Kyōsai." A shōjō is a mythical creature. Kyōsai means "crazy studio." Kawanabe was well-known for his bold artwork, humor, and modern, forward-thinking style. He paired political commentary with satire, which was not always well-received by the Japanese government. In 1870, he was arrested and beaten for painting obscene images. He didn't let that stop him though. In 1874, he helped create the first manga magazine.

Eshinbun Nipponchi, or *Illustrated News*, was a collaboration between journalist Robun Kanagaki and Kawanabe. They based it on a satirical illustrated magazine called *Japan Punch*, which was published by Englishman Charles Wirgman. *Japan Punch* was created for Western readers. *Eshinbun Nipponchi* was for Japanese readers. But the magazine lasted only three issues. It had a simple art style that didn't catch on. Other people tried creating similar magazines using their own style. These magazines were written and illustrated with adult readers in mind. The text was often related to Japanese issues and events, and the art was inspired by Chinese graphic art styles.

Magazines for Everyone

In 1895, Japanese book publishers began creating magazines for separate audiences. The Japanese government wanted children to have a sense of nationalism and for them to find their place in society. A Japanese publisher who made books for kids realized that comics might appeal to their target audience—boys. *Shōnen Sekai*, or *Boy's World*, used cartoons to tell stories with moral tales meant to encourage Japanese pride. A girl's version, called *Shojo Kai*, or *Girl's Kingdom*, began publication in 1902.

The same year that *Shōnen Sekai* launched, a magazine called *Box of Curios* hired a professional cartoonist named Rakuten Kitazawa. The magazine was an English-language magazine that was published in Tokyo, Japan. Kitazawa was already an experienced cartoonist. He had been drawing editorial and political cartoons since the age of twelve. He expanded his knowledge of Western-style cartooning at *Box of Curios*.

Four years later, he was hired by a Japanese newspaper called *Jiji Shinpō*. The cartoonist he was replacing had been calling comics and cartoons manga, and Kitazawa began doing the same. In 1902, he created a short narrative-style comic strip that he called *Jiji Manga*. For the first time, Japanese comics had recurring main characters.

Kitazawa started editing a satirical magazine called *Tokyo Puck* in 1905. It was based on an American magazine called *Puck*. *Tokyo Puck* was Japan's first color manga magazine and quickly became popular. It was also translated into Chinese and English. It was so popular that for a while, any Japanese cartoons, manga, or comics were all called puck. *Tokyo Puck* made Kitazawa a household name. Some people even call him the Father of Manga. He encouraged fellow manga artists, growing the industry and its fame.

Comic strips were gaining traction in the United States too. Newspapers had been publishing comics before 1893, but that was the year full-color Sunday comics were first printed. Morrill Goddard, the Sunday editor of the *New York World*, imagined the Sunday comics, with essays, verses, and cartoons, as being like the paper's own magazine. The comics were a special insert of the Sunday papers.

By the 1920s, the comic strips had turned into story tidbits that readers looked forward to reading each week. They were finally reprinted in magazine form—as comic books—in the 1930s. The books were exported to other countries, including China, Korea, and Japan. Editor Ippei Okamoto began syndicating American cartoons in Japan, and he encouraged Japanese artists to find inspiration in them for their own styles.

War Means Changes

World War II (1939–1945) continued to change media in Japan. In 1947, the new Japanese Constitution outlawed any form of censorship. However, the presence of Allied soldiers in the country was its own form of censorship. The US military reviewed every publication and had a list of topics that were forbidden. Japanese people had less disposable income to spend on reading too. Inexpensive, longer manga stories called *akahon*, or "red books," were printed and sold in neighborhood shops.

Astro Boy has been a beloved figure for decades. The character is so popular that he was even featured on a postage stamp.

In 1951, Osamu Tezuka created one of the most influential manga—and later anime—in the world. *Tetsuwan Atom*, or *Astro Boy* in English, was meant to give Japanese children hope for the future. In a sci-fi world of rockets and skyscrapers were also rundown houses that post-war Japanese children could identify. Tezuka's art style, which was inspired by American cartoon characters such as Mickey Mouse and Betty Boop, included characters with large eyes, which would become a staple of manga.

Astro Boy was published from 1952 to 1968 in Kodansha's *Weekly Shōnen Magazine*, which was the first weekly manga magazine. By the time the story was finished, *Astro Boy*

Manga in Other Parts of the World

Globalization has given people around the world the chance to experience manga in their own language. South Korean manhwa and Chinese/Taiwanese manhua are finding their place on the international market too. Like manga, manhwa and manhua often draw on their own countries' histories and culture. They commonly come in full color. Manhwa and manhua are often released as webtoons, which do not fall within regular book page sizes. Instead, the reader progresses through the story by scrolling. Some manhwa and manhua might get a printed version later.

ended up being more than five thousand pages long. Tezuka was a widely known figure in Japan. He had illustrated children's books, both men's and women's magazines, and political cartoons. He showed Japanese people that being a manga artist was a legitimate occupation. Although the *Astro Boy* anime, which came out in 1963, was incredibly popular in the United States, the original manga didn't get a printed English translation until 2002.

A Favorite Pastime

In the 1960s, manga started to grow exponentially. The Japanese economy was beginning to bounce back, which meant people had more money to spend. More affordable art supplies gave more people the chance to draw their own manga. Japanese people also loved reading.

Otaku Culture

English-speaking anime and manga fans might recognize the words *otaku* or *weeb* as descriptive terms for people who love anime and manga. Otaku culture was first recognized in the 1970s and 1980s as anime and manga began finding hardcore fans. Later, *otaku* took on a more negative meaning for the socially awkward, obsessive, or delusional. In recent years, it has become a positive thing again.

Otaku culture introduces new fans to Japanese media and society. Otaku from all over the world travel to Tokyo to buy products related to their favorite series and attend conventions. The Japanese government even has an industry term for it—contents tourism.

Fans of anime and manga can attend conventions and other events dressed as their favorite characters.

In a 1968 survey, reading was chosen as the top recreational and leisure activity. As an island nation that had never been colonized—so it only had one common language—and that believed in universal education, Japan had an incredibly high literacy rate. Even poorer people could afford to rent a book from one of the thousands of book lenders across the country. Many monthly magazines switched to being released weekly. People viewed a career in manga as well-respected and socially acceptable, and also as a pursuit that could come with fame and reward.

Women in Manga

Manga had traditionally been a primarily male-driven artform. Overly feminine or simplistic, one-dimensional female characters were common. Even manga drawn for women and girls was created by men. But in the 1960s, more women began entering the field. They took over shojo manga. Finally, stories that represented the female experience were available.

Later, josei manga, which was for older female readers, gained a foothold too. Female writers began making a name for themselves in shonen manga as well. Hiromu Arakawa's *Fullmetal Alchemist* and Rumiko Takahashi's *InuYasha* are just two examples. Daniel Flis, writing for The Japan Foundation, Sydney [Australia], said, "Female authors writing in the shonen genre are more likely to critique or subvert the dominant gendered framework than male authors." Manga would be changed forever.

CHAPTER TWO

On the Next Episode of . . .

Anime dates back to the early 1900s. Early anime was silent and five minutes or shorter. Music played in the theater and a narrator, called a benshi, told the audience what was happening. Unfortunately, a common practice at the time was to dismantle films after they were used. Other reels degraded over time. There is not much left to give us a deeper look at early anime. One surviving clip believed to be from 1907 is three seconds long. The clip's fifty frames show a boy dressed as a sailor.

Japan's original three animators were Oten Shimokawa, Junichi Kouchi, and Seitaro Kitayama. They all had works created around 1916 to 1917, and they all worked independently of each other. Shimokawa's film *Imokawa Muzuko*, or *The Janitor*, is believed to be the first commercially released animated film, although no copies survive to prove it. In total, Shimokawa made perhaps five films. His main work was as a cartoonist for the satirical *Tokyo Puck*.

Kouchi was a watercolor painter and an employee at *Tokyo Puck*, working under Rakuten Kitazawa. In 1917, he was hired

Dull Sword appears yellow because it was originally restored on yellow-tinted nitrate plates.

by Kobayashi Shokai, an entertainment company, to animate a short film called *Namakura Gatana*, or *Dull Sword*. He made two other films for them before returning to newspaper cartooning. In 1923, he founded Sumikazu, his own animation studio, and created some propaganda videos for the Japanese government. His final film was *Cut Up Serpent* in 1931.

Kitayama was a painter and an art magazine editor. He founded the very first anime studio, Kitayama Eiga Seisakujo, in 1921. In 2024, one of Kitayama's earliest films, *Dental Health*, was discovered. It emphasized the importance of good diet and dental care. Kitayama was also a fan of Western art and supported young artists by buying them art supplies. He displayed and published their works.

Destruction Leads to Rebuilding

In 1923, an enormous earthquake shocked Tokyo. A tsunami followed, and then fires swept across the city's wooden buildings. In the end, around 140,000 people died. Businesses were destroyed. And many works of art—including anime—

Age-Old Anime

Namakura Gatana is a four-minute cartoon about a samurai who buys a dull sword. It is not the first anime ever made. But the 1923 earthquake meant many original works were lost, and *Namakura Gatana* was one of the few surviving pieces. Animators bounced back from this loss, and in 1943, *Momotarō no Umiwashi*, or *Momotarō's Sea Eagles*, was released. It was nearly feature-length at thirty-seven minutes long. The movie showed a human fighting alongside cute animals. The propaganda film was commissioned by the Japanese Navy.

The National Museum of Modern Art, Tokyo, built a website to share the beginnings of Japanese animation. Sixty-four short films made between 1917 and 1941 can be watched with or without subtitles.

More than half of the brick buildings in Tokyo were destroyed as a result of the 1923 earthquake.

were lost.

American cartoons were shown around the world in the 1920s and 1930s. This golden age of animation led to new innovations and feature-length movies. They even became part of war propaganda. But in Japan, animation did not get the same resources to advance. The country was still recovering after the earthquake.

Many studios had been destroyed, and people were still rebuilding their lives and their businesses. It was hard for animators to get funding for new projects, especially since most of them worked independently. Small studios also couldn't compete with Disney, which had huge numbers of employees, big budgets, and the resources to make full-color movies with sound.

But Japanese animators didn't stop working, and in fact, used American animation as inspiration. Plots began taking on Western-style humor and pacing rather than relying on more traditional folktales.

During World War II, the Japanese government used animation for its benefit. Many propaganda and instructional films were made during this time, leading to growth in the industry. The most well-known movie from this time was

For years, it was believed that all copies of *Momotarō: Sacred Sailors* had been destroyed by US forces. But a single copy was found in 1983.

Momotarō: Umi no Shinpei, or *Momotarō: Sacred Sailors*, Japan's first feature-length animated film at seventy-four minutes. It was finished in 1945 and was a sequel to *Momotarō's Sea Eagles*.

The animation was as technically sophisticated as anything in America and it featured machines in incredible detail, which would later inspire the mecha robots that would become a signature of Japanese anime. Unfortunately, the film's release was delayed, and rather than being a dramatic celebration of Japan's military might and heroism, it was a reminder of Japan's failure.

Astro Boy

Japan Animated Films was founded in 1948, and in 1956, it was acquired by Toei Company as its animation department. It would be the first anime production company in the country. In 1958, it released the first feature-length, full-color anime movie, *Hakujaden*, or *The Tale of the White Serpent*. Toei would go on to produce more feature-length anime movies and TV shows, such as *Dragon Ball*, *ONE PIECE*, and *Sailor Moon*.

In 1963, the popular manga *Astro Boy* was turned into an anime. Author Osamu Tezuka, who had worked at Toei, left to start his own animation studio called Mushi Production. In order to cut costs, the studio came up with measures that became staples of new age anime, such as still frames and repeated scenes. Astro Boy's big eyes made it easier for people to see Astro Boy's emotions and to forget he was a robot. Other anime, such as *Sailor Moon* and *ONE PIECE*, followed this example.

When TV networks in the United States agreed to show *Astro Boy*, the show required even more trimming for American audiences. Names were changed and scenes were cut. Anything remotely Japanese or that might be seen as too violent was removed. But even so, it was incredibly popular. It was America's first exposure to Japanese culture. Even today, the *Astro Boy* theme song can be heard at American sporting events.

Rebuilding and Re-Creating

Astro Boy's success led to Toei creating the first shojo anime in 1966. *Mahotsukai Sally*, or *Sally the Witch*, was successful around the world. And in 1967, *Mach GoGoGo*, or *Speed Racer*, sped through Japanese and American households, bringing action, adventure, and comedy together for fans of all ages.

In the 1970s, several production companies split. Some employees got together to start Nippon Animation. They found fame adapting classic stories from around the world, including *Arabian Nights* and *Anne of Green Gables*, which were easy sells to other countries.

In 1979, *Mobile Suit Gundam* introduced TV watchers to giant robots, and *Doraemon*, a comedy series based on manga, got an update. *Doraemon* ran for 1,787 episodes. The show ended in 2005 but was rebooted a month later with updated designs and new voice actors. Manga, movies, action figures, and video games made anime even more popular.

Golden Era in Animation

The 1980s are considered the golden age of anime. It finally

Hayao Miyazaki grew up in post-World War II Japan. Many of his movies have themes of environmentalism, friendship, and pacifism.

had a strong foothold in TV. Now it was time to return to the big screen. Hayao Miyazaki created a film version of *Nausicaä of the Valley of the Wind* based on a magazine comic printed by Tokuma Shoten, a major publisher in Japan. *Nausicaä* was such a huge success that Tokuma Shoten financed a full animation studio, Studio Ghibli. Miyazaki went on to create hits such as *My Neighbor Totoro*, *Kiki's Delivery Service*, and *Spirited Away*. He also worked with friend and fellow filmmaker Isao Takahata on movies such as *Grave of the Fireflies* and *Pom Poko*. Studio Ghibli films are some of the highest-grossing films in Japan.

Toei turned Akira Toriyama's *Dragon Ball* into an anime in 1986. It blended humor and action and introduced many story elements that are now common tropes in anime and manga—the theme of passing the torch, tournament arcs,

Healing Magic

By 2019, anime—including shows, movies, and merchandise—was a $24-billion business. Experts assumed the anime industry would suffer during the 2020 COVID-19 pandemic, but although there was a drop, presumably because movie theaters were closed and big crowds were forbidden, streaming numbers were up. By 2023, the market was nearing $29 billion, with an expected increase of more than 10 percent by 2030. And fans around the world clamored for new shows. Thanks to *Demon Slayer: Mugen Train*, 2020 was the third-highest-grossing year the anime industry had ever seen.

shifting genres, and training to power up, to name a few. Five different iterations of *Dragon Ball* entertained watchers for decades.

The film *Akira* was released in 1988. It showed that Japan was finally ready to throw money into producing top-tier anime. Its smooth animation, rich colors, and attention to detail was created without any computers. The voice-overs were prerecorded, which allowed the animators to draw around the dialogue instead of having the actors try to match dialogue to already-existing animations. Considered by some to be the greatest anime of all time, *Akira* has inspired filmmakers around the globe for decades.

Anime around the World

The Japanese economy crashed in 1991, leading to many

Studio Ghibli's popularity led to the creation of Ghibli Park in Nagakute, Japan. Park visitors can interact with larger-than-life characters and scenery from Studio Ghibli films, such as No-Face from *Spirited Away*.

studios shutting their doors. But Studio Ghibli persevered, and TV shows continued to be popular. *Sailor Moon* debuted in Japan in 1992 and in North America in 1995. Two years later, *Pokémon* aired in Japan. It reached the United States in 1998 and became a global phenomenon. Anime was becoming mainstream in homes around the world.

In 2002, Studio Ghibli's *Spirited Away* won the Golden Bear award at the Berlin International Film Festival. The next year, it took home an Academy Award for Best Animated Feature. No non-American film had ever won this honor. It brought in new viewers who had never seen anime before and impressed people who were already fans. It showed that anime was more than cartoons for kids. "I believe that stories have an important role to play in the formation of human beings," director Hayao Miyazaki said. "They can stimulate, amaze, and inspire their listeners."

CHAPTER THREE

It's Your Destiny

Manga and anime are more than just comic books and cartoons. There are many different genres, storytelling styles, and art styles to appeal to any reader, no matter their age, gender, or interests. Visit your local library or bookstore and check out all the different subjects that books come in. Some books may belong in two—or even more!—categories. It's the same for anime and manga.

Demographics

In the 1950s and 1960s, manga was split into two main categories: shojo and shonen. Today, they are further broken down by age and gender: shojo and josei, shonen and seinen, and more. Each type shares similarities and differences with the others. These breakdowns aren't specific genres. Instead, they describe their intended audiences. Let's check out the benefits of some of the categories.

Some vintage shojo manga are worth hundreds of US dollars.

Shojo

Shojo stories focus on human relationships, whether they be between friends, lovers, or even between humans and ghosts. Emotions and feelings dominate the plotlines, especially feelings of love and friendship.

Osamu Tezuka's *Ribon no Kishi* (*Princess Knight*) was the first manga for girls with a Japanese storyline. It was first published in 1966. The main character, Sapphire, is born a girl but raised as a boy. She uses her alter ego, Princess Knight, to fight enemies and defend the throne. The manga was heavily inspired by a form of Japanese theater that only used young women as actors. Feminine male characters and women who dress as men are common shojo tropes.

Sailor Moon, created by Naoko Takeuchi, was an introduction to anime for many Western audiences. The manga ran from 1991 to 1998. The anime began in 1992 but didn't get a North American release until 1995. Much of the content was Americanized, erasing a lot of the Japanese culture and shojo aspects. But its popularity paved the way for other anime to be adapted for Western audiences.

Cardcaptor Sakura is a classic magical girl shojo by an all-female artist team known as CLAMP. It ran from 1996 to 2000, with a sequel released in 2016. There was also an anime, which aired as *Cardcaptors* in North America. The story follows Sakura Kinomoto, who accidentally releases magical cards into the world and must track them all down. The manga's portrayal of young love and diverse gender roles earned it praise when it was released and is still appreciated today.

Other well-known shojo works include *Fruits Basket*, *Princess Jellyfish*, *Kimi ni Todoke*, *The Rose of Versailles*, *Ouran High School Host Club*, *In the Clear Moonlit Dusk*, and *A Sign of Affection*.

Shonen

The stories that drive shonen are usually more lighthearted and less serious. They are full of action and adventure. Sometimes, the hero must go on a quest. Other times, they set out to prove themselves to others by defeating enemies. They make friends along the way. In 2024, *Weekly Shonen*

Jump was the best-selling and longest-running shonen magazine in the world, with more than 7.5 billion copies sold since it first started in 1968. In September 2022, it broke a Guinness World Record, with an average weekly circulation of 1.28 million copies. Adding digital copies, that's nearly two million a week.

Four shonen manga and anime have become the main staples among audiences. *Dragon Ball*, *BLEACH*, *Naruto*, and *ONE PIECE* have inspired many other manga and anime in this category. They all started in *Weekly Shonen Jump*.

Dragon Ball was created by Akira Toriyama in 1984. It went on to have two manga series, five anime, twenty-one movies, and more than one hundred video games. The story of Goku and his friends searching for Dragon Balls, fighting villains, and seeing who can become the strongest martial artist in the universe has resonated with fans of all ages. Even though Toriyama passed away in March 2024, the quest continues, as Toriyama left storylines behind, and manga artist Toyotarou has taken over illustration duties.

Fans have been following the adventures of Monkey D. Luffy and his Straw Hat Pirates as they search for the One Piece since 1997. Eiichiro Oda's tale was the best-selling manga series between 2008 and 2018. In July 2022, it broke the record for the most copies published for the same comic book series by a single author. *ONE PIECE* has also been turned into films, anime, games, and a live-action series.

Masashi Kishimoto first published *Naruto* in 1999. The story of Naruto's quest for recognition and acceptance became an anime in 2002. The manga went until 2014, spanning seven hundred chapters and inspiring a sequel series, *Boruto*. *Naruto* has sold more than 250 million copies worldwide.

Hundreds of anime episodes, nearly a dozen movies, and various forms of manga publication have reached fans in ninety countries. In September 2024, a first printing of the manga's first volume sold for $20,000 at an auction.

BLEACH was created by Tite Kubo and first published in 2001. Teenager Ichigo Kurosaki is granted the power of a Soul Reaper, which he uses to protect humans and help spirits reach the afterlife. It was rereleased as seventy-four tankōbon volumes, and has had an anime series, movies, stage musicals, video games, and a live-action movie.

Other well-known shonen works include *Chainsaw Man*, *Jujutsu Kaisen*, *Gintama*, *Fullmetal Alchemist*, and *Wind Breaker*.

Josei

Josei stories tend to be more mature, concentrating around adult relationships, workplaces, and other life events. But some also focus on high school students. The first magazine for this audience was *Be Love*, which was first printed in 1980.

Romance is one of the fastest-growing areas in publishing. As readers age out of shojo and look for more mature, adult relationships, josei stories are there to fill that gap. Will-they, won't-they stories are a common trope in keeping romance manga and anime going. In the 2000s, more shojo and josei were turned into anime, making them more popular than ever.

Some popular josei include *Kakuriyo*, *NANA*, *Yuri!!! On Ice*, *Chihayafuru*, and *Wotakoi: Love is Hard for Otaku*.

Naruto has been on the *New York Times* bestseller list multiple times.

Seinen

Seinen stories often feature students at universities or men at work. They also touch on politics, sci-fi, relationships, sports, and more. The first seinen magazines came about in the late 1960s as fans who grew up during shonen manga's rise in the 1950s grew older. One of the first seinen-specific magazines was *Weekly Manga Action*.

There is some crossover between shonen and seinen. For example, some might see *One-Punch Man* as a shonen because of the fight scenes, but others might see its more mature humor and story themes resonate with older readers.

Other well-known seinen include *Lupin III*, *Witch Hat Atelier*, *March Comes in Like a Lion*, and *Kaguya-Sama: Love is War*.

Kodomo

In Japanese, the term *kodomo* means "children," and that's kodomo manga and anime's targeted audience—readers age ten or under. Simpler stories, less action, and lessons learned at the end of the chapter or episode are common in kodomo manga and anime. For a while, many manga and anime were considered kodomo, but a split became more evident as older people began watching and reading anime and manga too. *Astro Boy*, *Hello Kitty*, and *Doraemon* are all examples of kodomo. *Pokémon* is a more recent global example.

Gekiga

Gekiga are stories meant for adult audiences. They have more mature themes and tend to be highly realistic. Gekiga has challenged the status quo in Japan since the 1950s. It stepped away from tropes and romanticism to tackle harder subjects

Predictable Fun

Anime and manga are full of tropes that have become commonplace, even in Western media. Here are a few of the more common ones.

- Magical Girls: Teenage girls are given special powers that allow them to transform and get new abilities that they use to fight crime.
- Giant Swords: An unrealistically large sword is bigger than its user.
- Harems: The main character is surrounded by multiple potential romantic partners.
- Truck-kun: Common especially in isekai, characters are hit by a truck and are sent to the afterlife or to a supernatural or other type of realm.
- Leveling Up: The hero is able to unlock a new power just in time to beat the bad guy.
- Toast of Tardiness: The main character grabs a piece of toast and runs with it in her mouth to show she's running late.

such as anti-government sentiments, morality, and adult relationships. Its development was similar to how graphic novels such as Alan Moore's *Watchmen* and Art Spiegelman's *Maus* stemmed from Western comic books. The "man protecting a child on a dangerous journey" trope dates back to a gekiga created by Kazuo Koike.

Shop to It

Anime and manga can be found in all sorts of surprising places! Licensing deals bring popular characters to everyday items. *Hello Kitty*- and *Pokémon*-branded items are fairly common. But shoppers might be surprised to find *Naruto* ramen or *Sailor Moon* sparkling water. In 2024, McDonald's made a special *Jujutsu Kaisen* garlic sauce, but the show had also marketed to a different audience when they partnered with the fashion company Dolce & Gabbana in 2022. In 2024, Puma sold *ONE PIECE* shoes and Crocs had *Demon Slayer* designs.

Genres

Anime and manga come in a huge variety of genres. Some can be categorized under two or more genres—for example, an adventure manga might take place in the past and involve a couple who like each other solving crimes together. There's no official list of genres, and categorizing anime and manga within them can be totally subjective. Here are some examples of genres and series that fall under them.

Sports

Slam Dunk, Haikyu!!, Ace of Diamond

Cooking

Yakitate Japan!!, Restaurant to Another World, Delicious in Dungeon

Action/Adventure

JoJo's Bizarre Adventure, Fullmetal Alchemist, Hunter x Hunter

Samurai

Rurouni Kenshin, The Elusive Samurai, Sengoku

Comedy

The Disastrous Life of Saiki K., Spy x Family, Gintama, Beck

Slice of Life

These stories generally focus on the everyday lives of their characters.

Fruits Basket, Ranma ½, NANA

Sci-Fi

Ghost in the Shell, Neon Genesis Evangelion, Battle Angel Alita

Supernatural

Tokyo Ghoul, Blue Exorcist, Demon Slayer, Kimetsu Yu Yu Hakusho

Isekai

Isekai is a genre where an everyday person is transported to a fantasy, game, or other type of world.

InuYasha, Sword Art Online, Digimon, Fushigi Yugi

CHAPTER FOUR

Spoiler Alert

Once, people saw anime and manga as a niche form of entertainment. They were things you were into if you were Japanese or if you were very interested in Japanese culture. It might be something you watched if you were up late at night or if you liked reading or watching TV on your desktop computer. People who liked video games might also like it because many of the games they played came from Japan. Parents might read or watch it because their kids did. But as it became more mainstream, more people got interested.

Between 2019 and 2022, manga sales in the United States quadrupled. At its height, 28.4 million copies of manga books were purchased, shared, and enjoyed. In 2024, it was the fourth-most-popular fiction category. Romance, thrillers, and fantasy were the top three. Celebrities, including rapper Megan Thee Stallion and football player Jamaal Williams, call themselves certified anime nerds. In 2023, the Los Angeles Chargers introduced their game schedule as an anime. And references to well-known anime and manga—and sometimes

ONE PIECE **was originally meant to end in 2002, but Oda realized he had more story to tell.**

more niche tropes—make it to mainstream American TV shows, such as *Jeopardy* and *The Simpsons*.

Record Setters

Eiichiro Oda's *ONE PIECE* reached the milestone of being the most popular manga of all time in 2008. It sold 516.6 million copies between December 1997 and September 2022.

As of July 2024, there were more than one thousand chapters divided into 109 tankōbon volumes, making it the twenty-first-longest manga series. Oda said he planned to end the series sometime in 2024 or 2025. The anime has been nearly as long-running, beginning in 1999 and airing for more than twenty-five years.

The longest-running anime of all time is *Sazae-san*, created by Machiko Hasegawa (1920–1992) in 1946. Hasegawa was Japan's first successful female manga artist. First appearing in newspapers as a four-panel comic strip, the slice of life manga followed Sazae-san, a housewife who takes care of her family every day. It may seem much more mundane than dramatic shonen fights or cute will-they, won't-they shojo, but the wholesome content and fuzzy familiarity have helped its popularity span generations.

As Japan's best-loved comic strip, *Sazae-san* captured the hearts of readers without having any superpowers, magic, or charms. They liked Sazae-san's quirky sense of humor and positive spirit. *Sazae-san* was published as sixty-eight paperbacks that have sold more than sixty-eight million copies. Its anime began in 1969 and earned the Guinness World Record in 2023 for longest-running animated TV series, with more than 2,250 episodes.

Spend Money to Make Money

The more popular anime becomes, the more studios are willing to spend on production. The average animated show costs between $60,000 and $100,000 per episode to produce. Larger numbers of workers, special effects, voice actors, and music are only a few things that drive up the cost. *Dragon Ball*

Machiko Hasegawa made her manga debut at the age of fourteen.

Super, a saga part of Akira Toriyama's *Dragon Ball* franchise, cost $170,000 per episode in 2024, making it the most expensive anime ever made. Its two full-length films, *Dragon Ball Super: Broly* and *Dragon Ball Super: Super Hero*, both made it to the top twenty in highest-grossing anime films of all time, with *Super Hero* bringing in more than $86.6 million.

But an anime doesn't necessarily need to be a big-ticket show to find long-term success. *Neon Genesis Evangelion* famously blew its budget on elaborate fight scenes, forcing the rest of the show to recycle animation and rely on simpler art and still shots. The last two episodes needed a complete rewrite, which caused the show to have a vague, inconclusive ending. But even today, the show is consistently listed in top-ten and top-twenty lists. Its production studio, Gainax, went on to create some other popular shows, such as *FLCL* and *Nadia: The Secret of Blue Water.* But the company had been struggling for years despite that success, and in 2024, it filed for bankruptcy.

Neon Genesis Evangelion is a complex, mature story full of symbolism. *KochiKame*, also known as *Kochira Katsushika-ku Kameari Koen Mae Hashutsujo*, or *KochiKame: Tokyo Beat Cops*, is the complete opposite. Created by Osamu Akimoto, it made its first appearance in *Weekly Shonen Jump* in 1976. The main character is a police officer who is always trying to find his next get-rich-quick scheme. The simple, funny plots meant that new fans could jump right in without needing to know a lot of backstory. By the time it ended in 2016, there were 1,960 chapters published in 201 volumes, making it the longest-running manga series in history.

Everybody's Favorite Pocket Monsters

When anime and manga become popular, fans will do anything to get their hands on items featuring their favorite characters. *Pokémon* is the highest-grossing anime franchise in the world. It began in 1996 with the video games *Pokémon Red* and *Pokémon Blue*. An anime that adapted the plot of the games quickly followed. Collecting Pokémon, battling gym leaders, and exploring the Kanto region and beyond were storytelling devices that were popular across both mediums. The first movie made nearly $173 million worldwide.

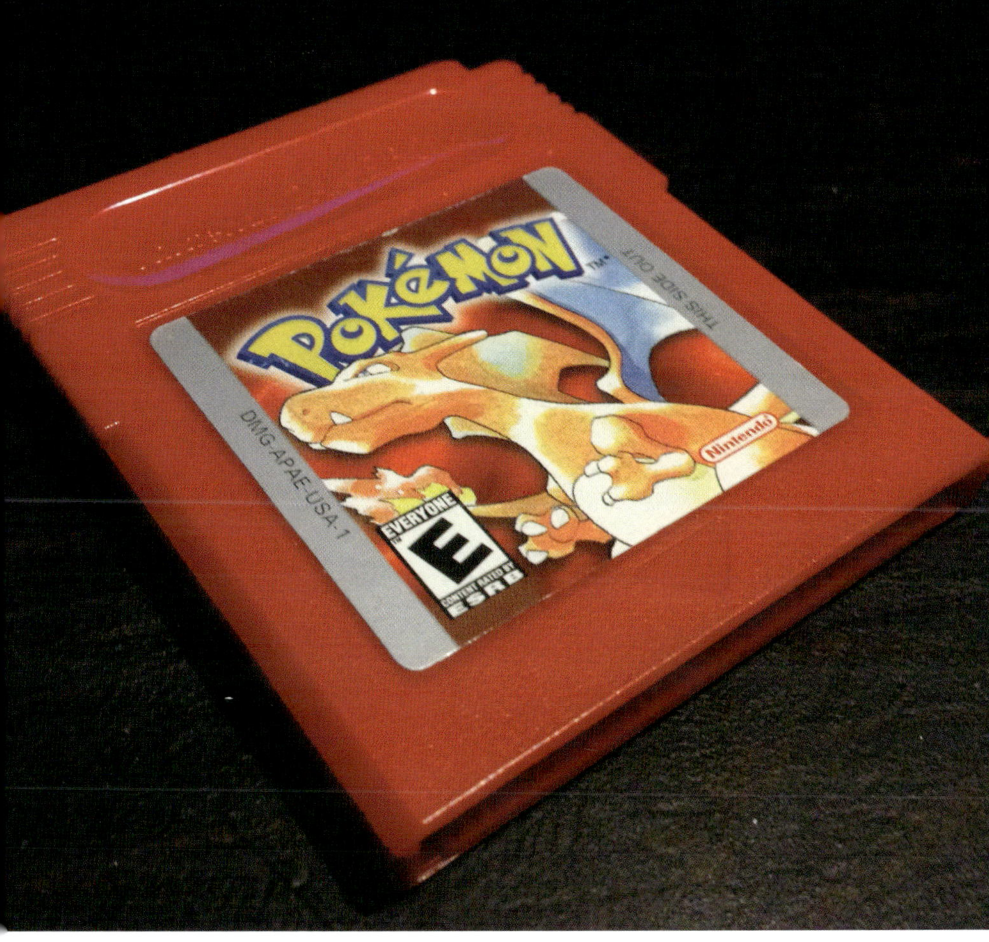

The original *Pokémon* games, which were made for the Nintendo Game Boy sold nearly 31.5 million copies worldwide.

Pokémon takes full advantage of licensing deals to increase its value. A line of products for babies and young children called monpoké includes picture books, clothing, and plushies. A Pokémon Sleep app helps people track their sleep and rewards them with Pokémon. There are also related tie-in products, such as pajamas, bedding, eye masks, and a Pokémon-printed mattress. The brand has even partnered with high-end companies such as Tiffany & Co. and FENDI. By 2024, the franchise had made $105 billion in revenue.

Where to Watch

Today, anime can be found on popular streaming services such as Netflix and Amazon Prime. Manga can be found in bookstores and at the library. In the recent past though, options were much more limited. *Shonen Jump* wasn't published in North America until November 2002, and unlike the Japanese version, it was released every month, not every week.

One way people read manga outside of Japan was through scanlations, also called "raws." Amateur fans scanned, translated, and edited manga without permission from the publishing companies, although the authors sometimes gave their approval. The first scanlations date back to the 1970s. Because this was pre-internet, they were limited to closed groups who distributed them offline.

In the 1990s, people could download raws on websites and get updates on releases. Large groups of people began to collaborate. By the 2000s, there was a shift from the original intent of translating harder-to-find manga meant to introduce new readers. Now it was a source for people to read popular manga for free. In the 2010s, publishers in both Japan and North America began to go after scanlation sites, and most shut down.

A similar process was used for anime. People exchanged pirated VHSs and DVDs in the 1980s and 1990s through the mail or at fan conventions. Sometimes, bootleg copies could be found at comic book stores or Asian markets. There were even mail-delivery services for bootleg anime. They were untranslated and often poor quality.

In 1997, Toonami, which was owned by Cartoon Network, began airing anime, including *Sailor Moon*, *Dragon Ball Z*, *Ronin Warriors*, and *G-Force: Guardians of Space*. Later, it broadcasted *Gundam Wing*, with the edited version during the day and the unedited one at night, setting up the introduction of more adult anime. But watching Toonami required cable television, something only mostly suburban and middle-class families had.

File-sharing sites built to distribute video files grew popular in the early 2000s. Sharing these files was called torrenting. Internet speeds were much slower though, and it could take a whole night—or several days—to download a low-quality file. Some licensed versions could be found at video stores or even mainstream outlets such as Best Buy, but they were expensive and it was hard to complete a set.

In 2024, Crunchyroll was the most popular streaming service for anime. It has the largest variety and releases new episodes as simulcasts with Japan. Users can filter between original language anime with English subtitles (subs) or watch the show with English voice actors (dubs).

More than fifteen million people subscribe to Crunchyroll, which features around 1,300 series and more than 46,000 episodes.

CHAPTER FIVE

Choose Your Main Character

People enjoy manga in many different ways. In Japan, manga cafés exist as a place for manga lovers to read a wide variety of manga for a small fee. They also have free Wi-Fi and drinks as well as cheap food, and some even allow guests to stay overnight. The first manga café outside of Japan opened in 2006 in Paris, France, but they have been popping up all over the world, including in South America and the Middle East.

Manga cafés haven't quite caught on in the same way in the United States, but the country is one of the largest importers of manga. Many countries in Europe, including Italy, France, and Germany, have begun importing it as well. Brazil is one of the biggest markets outside of Asia, with the largest Japanese population outside of Japan. In Mexico, the shared family values and narrative similarities between anime and telenovelas made Japanese media instantly popular.

AnimeJapan is held at the Tokyo Big Sight exhibition center.

Offline Adventures

The biggest anime convention in the world takes place in Japan every year. In 2023, AnimeJapan—formerly the Tokyo International Anime Fair—celebrated its tenth anniversary, welcoming more than 100,000 manga and anime lovers, cosplayers, exhibitors, and guest speakers. The next year, more than 132,500 people attended. It is one of the largest anime-centric conventions in the world. Anime and foreign film production companies, as well as toy, software, and game developers, all attend. Fans get to see anime trailers and hear announcements about their favorite shows.

In Paris, Japan Expo brings manga artists, illustrators, musicians, and other creators together. Fans can attend workshops to learn how to draw manga or try traditional activities such as origami or calligraphy. Those interested in cosplay can attend classes to learn how to make their own. People can test out video games, and esports tournaments pit the best players against each other. Special screenings of anime previews get fans excited for the next season of their favorite shows. Japan Expo was the first event in the world with a cosplay-specific stage, and more than fourteen thousand people show up to cheer on their favorite cosplayers each year.

In North America, anime and manga fans flock to Anime Expo, also known as AX, in Los Angeles, California. It was started in 1991 by students at UC Berkeley who had already formed an anime club. In 2001, more than ten thousand people traveled to the event. Three years later, that number had increased to twenty-five thousand. In 2016, more than 100,000 showed up. That number jumped to more than 392,000 in 2024, making it the largest anime convention in North America.

On Exhibit

As manga for young readers became more popular, people started to forget that manga is art first. In modern times, art

The Kawasaki City Museum holds more than eighty thousand pieces related to manga.

museums are showcasing both historical and contemporary manga. The Kawasaki City Museum opened in 1988 as the first public museum with a manga collection. Dedicated to the work of Fujiko F. Fujio, the creator of *Doraemon*, it displays original drawings, tools, and a huge library of *Doraemon* manga.

In the 1990s, artists began holding manga exhibitions at museums or public spaces. Sometimes, the exhibitions were multimedia, with videos, animation, or slideshows showcasing the artist's process or progression. In 2014, the Kyoto International Manga Museum exhibited eighteen thousand original drawings by Seiki Tsuchida. They were displayed in cases but also spread across the ground (under tempered glass) for full effect.

JAPAN HOUSE is a cultural center meant to promote Japanese culture, from art to food to film.

In 2019, JAPAN HOUSE Los Angeles displayed more than four hundred original drawings by Naoki Urasawa, a creator who has been called a modern-day Tezuka for his *Astro Boy*-inspired series, *Pluto*. The exhibition gave fans a view into his creative process through storyboards and sketches. Such exhibitions appeal not only to art fans, but to fans of anime and manga who might not be as familiar with contemporary art.

The Saitama Municipal Cartoon Art Museum is the first of its kind to fully dedicate itself to comics. It is in the former home of Rakuten Kitazawa and features some of the many cartoons created over his career. Fans can visit and get a look at early cartoons by one of the most impactful artists in Japan.

Academic Launchpad

The next generation of manga artists is just waiting to start their careers. Many colleges and universities around the world offer manga and anime courses. In 2021, the first high school manga studies department was founded, with its first classes starting in 2023. Students at Kumamoto Prefectural Takamori High School learn from professional manga artists. They study character creation, panel layouts, and other manga production skills.

Kyoto Seika University is the first—and only—full academic department for manga in Japan. Students can study five different areas: Character Design, Animation, Cartoon Art, Comic Art, and New Generation Manga. With the help of industry professionals, many students make their manga debut while still in school.

Immerse Yourself

Other serious fans can take anime and manga tours when they visit Japan. Guided tours let them see popular sites, such as animation studios and museums. They can visit anime theme parks such as Nijigen no Mori and Universal Studios Japan. Shopping centers such as Nakano Broadway or Otome Road cater to their needs. Fans of particular movies or shows can visit the Gundam Base Tokyo, Pokémon Center, or Ghibli Park.

An important thing for fans of anime and manga to remember is that, while they are part of Japanese culture, they are not *Japan*. They are forms of entertainment and can be a stepping stone to culture, folklore, and art. But the Japanese experience is so much more than that. There are thousands of years of rich history that the country has to share.

If you find a manga or anime that sparks your interest, dig deeper. Learn about what was happening in Japan when it was being written. Who was the author, and what was their life like? Did they put any of their personal experiences into their work? The more the overall culture is appreciated, the more fans can get out of their favorite manga and TV shows.

Nakano Broadway is a shopping area full of anime and manga goods.

Manga for Good

In April 2016, two magnitude 7 earthquakes hit the prefecture of Kumamoto. Seventy-five people died, and nearly 1,900 more were injured. They caused the most damage to the area ever recorded, destroying more than eight thousand buildings and severely damaging another twenty-six thousand. Eiichiro Oda, the author of *ONE PIECE*, grew up in Kumamoto. He vowed to help rebuild his hometown and launched ONE PIECE Kumamoto Revival Project. It was meant to inspire the recovery efforts and make people smile. During the four-year-long "Hinokuni Reconstruction Arc," statues of the Straw Hat Pirates were installed throughout the prefecture. Oda also donated ¥800 million (worth approximately $6.8 million USD in 2016) and drew art for local products and businesses. Videos showed Monkey D. Luffy and the rest of the pirates visiting Kumamoto, and a *ONE PIECE*-themed travel guide was published for tourists who made the pilgrimage to the prefecture.

The Monkey D. Luffy statue in Kumamoto City is located in front of the Kumamoto Prefectural Offices.

CONCLUSION

Finishing Touches

The future of manga and anime looks bright. Globalization has made them more accessible than ever, as demonstrated by fans popping up in places such as Nigeria, Cuba, and Saudi Arabia. The global market is expected to reach $41.5 billion by 2028, with a growth of more than 12 percent every year.

The world may be getting more modern, but the stories of heroes, adventurers, friends, and magic are rooted in tradition. Japanese manga and anime artists have their own distinctive, instantly recognizable style no matter where you are or what language the words are written or spoken in. The lighter word counts in manga make it more accessible and appealing to struggling readers, and the art makes the stories easy to follow. The long story arcs and consistent publication and episode release schedules give fans something to look forward to, and they can stick with a series for years, growing along with it. Those distinctive styles are what draw fans in and keep anime and manga unique.

Michiyuki Honma, the CEO and President of Pierrot Co.

Saudi Arabia's first comic con, the Saudi Comic Con, was held in 2017 in Jeddah, Saudi Arabia.

Ltd., has helped oversee the production of popular anime such as *BLEACH* and *Naruto*. Around 30 percent of the company's video sales come from overseas. There has been pushback to change animation to match Western standards. But Honma has spoken out against the idea. "If Japanese animation is bound by such restrictions on expression, there is no way that people overseas will want to watch it," he said. "Works that are a hit in Japan are also a hit overseas. I believe that we must not make the mistake of approaching anime production in the wrong way." Fans fall in love with a creator's vision.

Anime and manga fans continue to engage with their favorite stories through cosplays, events, and creating fan content.

Dulling that vision will dull the product for everyone.

Fans have proven to be open-minded when it comes to entertainment created outside their country of origin. They are looking for stories that resonate with them, no matter where they're made. "Compared to the 2000s, readers seem to be more omnivorous now," Ben Applegate, a director at Penguin Random House, said. "It just doesn't seem like this generation of readers cares that much about whether manga is only comics produced in Japan for a Japanese audience." More creators from outside of Japan means more manga and anime for everyone.

The hardest part is settling on a series. Once you've found one that sparks your interest, dive in. There's no going back!

GLOSSARY

alter ego: a person's alternate self

arc: an act or story within a larger storyline with a clear beginning, middle, and end

bootleg: illegal copies of something, such as comics, TV episodes, movies, or music recordings

branded: given a unique and immediately recognizable appearance that sets it apart from other products

convention: a meeting of people with similar interests

cosplay: dressing up as a character from a movie, book, or video game

franchise: a series of books, TV shows, or movies that have the same or similar names and are about the same characters or the same universe

genre: a style of a creative work

gross: the amount of money something earns before taxes and expenses are taken out

kanji: a system of Japanese writing that uses traditional Chinese characters

licensing: allowing the use of copyrighted or patented material by a person or company

literacy: the ability to read and write

mundane: ordinary

niche: a specialized part of the market for a certain kind of product or service

propaganda: information used to promote a political cause or point of view

reboot: to bring back a long-gone TV series or create a new one based on the older show

recurring: appearing multiple times

revenue: income made from the sale of goods and services

satire: the use of humor, irony, exaggeration, or ridicule to expose an issue, especially in politics or other current events

syndicate: the act of selling articles, photographs, television shows, and comic strips to other organizations so they can be published or shown to a new audience

telenovela: a Latin American soap opera

trailer: a commercial advertisement for a feature film or show

trope: an overused theme or device

tsunami: a series of waves caused by an underwater earthquake, explosion, or eruption

ukiyo-e: a Japanese art style that uses woodblock prints and paintings

whimsical: playfully quaint or amusing

SOURCE NOTES

7 "I manga'd those people.": Eike Exner, "Ten Myths about Manga History," Medium, November 1, 2021, https://medium.com/@eike.exner/ten-myths-about-manga-history-475e092c8878.

15 "Female authors writing . . . than male authors.": Daniel Flis, "Straddling the Line: How Female Authors are Pushing the Boundaries of Gender Representation in Shonen Manga," *New Voices in Japanese Studies*, July 2, 2018, https://newvoices.org.au/volume-10/straddling-the-line-how-female-authors-are-pushing-the-boundaries-of-gender-representation-in-japanese-shonen-manga/.

25 "I believe that . . . inspire their listeners.": Hayao Miyazaki, quoted in Tom Mes, "Hayao Miyazaki," *Midnight Eye*, January 7, 2002, http://www.midnighteye.com/interviews/hayao-miyazaki/.

53 "If Japanese animation . . . the wrong way.": Michiyuki Honma, quoted in Spencer Baculi, "'Naruto' and 'Bleach' Anime Studio President Rejects Idea That Anime Should Conform To Western Standards: 'If You Make Animation With That In Mind, It Will Become Increasingly Boring,'" Bounding Into Comics, April 22, 2024, https://boundingintocomics.com/anime/naruto-and-bleach-anime-studio-president-rejects-idea-that-anime-should-conform-to-western-standards-if-you-make-animation-with-that-in-mind-it-will-become-increasingly-boring/.

55 "Compared to the . . . a Japanese audience.": Ben Applegate, quoted in Deb Aoki, "Manga Was Marquee at San Diego Comic-Con," *Publishers Weekly*, July 27, 2023, https://www.publishersweekly.com/pw/by-topic/industry-news/trade-shows-events/article/92862-manga-was-marquee-at-san-diego-comic-con.html.

SELECTED BIBLIOGRAPHY

"Drawn to Inspire: The Impact of Manga and Anime." JAPAN HOUSE Los Angeles, August 16, 2019. https://www.japanhousela.com/articles/the-impact-of-manga-and-anime/.

"Ehon: The Origin of Manga." Google Arts and Culture. Accessed August 20, 2024. https://artsandculture.google.com/story/ehon-the-origin-of-manga-coleccion-bujalance/BwUBp1uhbRQVPQ?hl=en-US.

Guzzanti, Flor. "The Influence of Anime and Manga on Western Pop Culture." Rock & Art Cultural Outreach, June 7, 2024. https://www.rockandart.org/influence-anime-and-manga-western-pop-culture/.

"Manga: A Brief History in 12 Works." The British Museum, December 5, 2018. https://www.britishmuseum.org/blog/manga-brief-history-12-works.

Our Culture Mag & Partners. "The Role of Anime in Modern World Culture and Its Place in People's Lives." *Our Culture*, October 25, 2021. https://ourculturemag.com/2021/10/25/the-role-of-anime-in-modern-world-culture-and-its-place-in-peoples-lives/.

Yong, Ced. "Manga and Anime Culture in Japan: It's Everywhere!" WanderWisdom, May 24, 2024. https://wanderwisdom.com/travel-destinations/Japan-Manga-Anime-Culture.

FURTHER INFORMATION

Books

Bolte, Mari. *Exploring Anime: From Giant Robots to Moving Castles.* Minneapolis: Twenty-First Century Books, 2026.
Discover the history and secrets behind anime, from past to present.

Hairston, Marc, and Pamela Gossin. *Exploring Anime and Manga*. San Diego: ReferencePoint Press, 2025.
Examine the tools, techniques, and creators behind anime and manga.

Ozumi, Asuka. *How to Be a Manga Artist.* New York: Thames & Hudson, Inc., 2024.
This is the ultimate guide for aspiring manga artists.

Sattin, Samuel. *Kid's Guide to Anime & Manga: Exploring the History of Japanese Animation and Comics.* Philadelphia: RP Kids, 2023.
Learn more about the history and importance of anime and manga.

Studio Hard Deluxe. *Manga & Anime Digital Illustration Guide: A Handbook for Beginners.* Tokyo: Tuttle Publishing, 2023.
Twelve professional manga artists share pro tips and step-by-step lessons to help you create and design manga characters.

Websites

Anime Outline: 10 Steps to Make Your Own Manga or Comic Book
https://www.animeoutline.com/steps-to-make-your-own-manga/
Step-by-step instructions provide all the tips and tricks to making your own manga.

Britannica: Anime
https://www.britannica.com/art/anime-Japanese-animation
Learn more about anime's history, popularity, and future.

Britannica: Asia and the Manga
https://www.britannica.com/art/comic-strip/Asia-and-the-manga
Learn about manga's early days, how authors made it, and who they made it for.

Five Books: Best Manga for Children and Teens
https://fivebooks.com/best-books/best-manga-for-children-and-teens-oscar/
Get recommendations from others on what to read next!

West Virginia Library Services: History, Content and More About Manga
https://www.wvls.org/history-content-and-more-about-manga/
Dive into a crash course on manga and its history.

INDEX

ABOUT THE AUTHOR

Mari Bolte is a Korean-American writer and editor who lives in Minnesota with her family and a zoo of pets. She loves books in all formats, but has a special fondness for manhwa and manga.

PHOTO ACKNOWLEDGMENTS

Image credits: kuremo/Shutterstock, p. 5; Katsushika Hokusai/Wikimedia Commons, p. 7; Katsushika Hokusai/The Howard Mansfield Collection, Gift of Howard Mansfield, 1936/Metropolitan Museum of Art/Wikimedia Commons, p. 9; neftali/Shutterstock, p. 12; Yury Karamanenko/iStock Editorial/Getty Images, p. 14; Junichi Kouchi/Kobayashi Shokai/Wikimedia Commons, p. 17; Yokohama Central Library/Wikimedia Commons, p. 19; Mitsuyo Seo/Shochiku Doga Kenkyujo/Wikimedia Commons, p. 20; TOKUMA SHOTEN/Album/Newscom, p. 23; Tomohiro Ohsumi/Getty Images, p. 25; agustin.photo/Shutterstock, p. 27; YMBPhotography/Shutterstock, p. 31; UcigPhoto/Shutterstock, p. 37; Sankei Shinbun Co., Ltd./Wikimedia Commons, p. 39; PxHere, p. 41; Sharaf Maksumov/Shutterstock, p. 43; Morio Taga/Jiji Press Photo/Newscom, p. 45; TOSHIFUMI KITAMURA/AFP/Getty Images, p. 47; Chizhevskaya Ekaterina/Shutterstock, p. 48; kuremo/Shutterstock, p. 50; Koshiro K/Shutterstock, p. 51.

Cover image: Dedraw Studio/Shutterstock